# A Letter To Myself:
## THREE STEPS TO CONFRONTING FEAR, EMBRACING FAILURE, AND CELEBRATING SUCCESS

# DR. KATHERINE Y. BROWN

www.TrueVinePublishing.org

A Letter to Myself
Dr. Katherine Y. Brown

Published by True Vine Publishing Co.
810 Dominican Dr.
Nashville, TN 37228
www.TrueVinePublishing.org

ISBN: 978-1-962783-21-7 Paperback
ISBN: 978-1-962783-22-4 eBook

Printed in the United States of America—First printing

# Dedication

To Anthony, Sydney, Irving, and Robert,

The courage to face my fears, combat my failures, and navigate to success stemmed from being the best version of myself that I could be for you. I love you more than words could ever express. Always know that you are loved.

With all my heart,
Love, Mom

# TABLE OF CONTENTS

# INTRODUCTION

During a challenging phase of my life, I faced questions like "Who am I?" "Who am I becoming?" "What do I want?" and "What will be my true commitments?" These questions were more than inquiries; they generated responses that altered my life's path. I had hit a plateau in my career and felt uncertain about the future, and these questions helped break through my stagnation. I finally realized barriers. Can you guess what they were? Fear, failure, and success had each become a distinct force influencing my path. This took work to realize how impactful these three words meant in my life. It demanded time, reflection, and repetition in building new habits.

Often, there is a reliance on external sources for motivation, including friends, family, organizations, and even recognition through awards and accolades. These reliances can potentially lead to challenges, especially when external acknowledgment of efforts is absent. For some, lack of recognition and even lack of authentic friendships can result in feelings of loss, failure, and diminishing motivation to engage in activities that once had meaning or enjoyment.

Self-awareness is an ongoing process requiring consistent self-examination. It requires the courage to ask, "What do I want?" "What do I need?" "What will having this help me to achieve?" Even when the answers are difficult to confront or share. When we understand and meet our needs and aspirations, we can begin the groundwork for an authentic and self-directed life, leading to satisfaction and a sense of accomplishment.

So, why am I sharing this with you? The reason is simple yet profound. I've discovered the power of self-reflection, primarily through writing letters to myself, addressing my fears, acknowledging my failures as opportunities for growth, and having an optimistic mindset toward celebrating my successes even before they happen. This practice has been essential to my personal growth. My words, thoughts, and actions have power; yours do, too.

I believe the three letters I am encouraging you to write can be as impactful for you as they have been for me. I am going to provide you with three steps that you can implement starting today. The true power lies in your hands because you are the author. You determine the letter that you write. Take your time and have patience with the process. You are worth the effort and through this practice, you can discover a better version of yourself. This is a letter that is worth writing.

# THREE STEPS:

## CONFRONTING FEAR, EMBRACING FAILURE, CELEBRATING SUCCESS

It's easy to become overwhelmed by the competing priorities, tasks, and goals we choose to set for ourselves. Sometimes, we change directions, pursuing many aspirations simultaneously, realizing that little gets accomplished without intention and focus. Recognizing the need for clear, focused goals requires three steps: confronting fear, embracing failure, and celebrating success.

### Step 1: Confronting Fear

The first step is confronting fear. What are you afraid of that holds you back from pursuing your goals? Take this moment of introspection to understand yourself. Do your fears have power over you? Are these fears justified? Often, what we fear is less about external judgment and more about our internal dialogues. Are your fears based on reality, founded or unfounded, and do they restrict your growth?

There are many types of fear. Fears may include the fear of letting others down, how we are perceived, or even the fear of rejection, which all are often at the core of indecision. Getting to the root of fears is crucial.

## WHY DO CERTAIN THINGS MATTER TO YOU?

_____

_____

_____

_____

_____

_____

_____

_____

_____

_____

_____

_____

_____

_____

_____

_____

_____

_____

_____

_____

# ARE YOUR FEARS VALID OR HOLDING YOU BACK FROM YOUR TRUE POTENTIAL?

_____

_____

_____

_____

_____

_____

_____

_____

_____

_____

_____

_____

_____

_____

_____

_____

_____

_____

_____

_____

_____

Identifying your fears is the first step toward overcoming them. Remember, identifying, acknowledging, and understanding fear is not a weakness but an act of courage towards self-improvement.

*Step 2: Embracing Failure*

It is imperative that you reshape your thinking to embrace failure, not as a setback, but as a first attempt in learning. Reflect on what didn't work out and ask yourself, how you could have approached it differently? Learning from life experiences is the key to building resilience and stamina to try again.

Life is full of unexpected twists, turns, plans that don't work out, and people who don't follow through or meet our expectations. These are learning experiences that help you grow stronger and more resilient.

# IDENTIFY AT LEAST THREE SITUATIONS THAT YOU ENCOUNTERED THAT DID NOT GO AS PLANNED.

_____

_____

_____

_____

_____

_____

_____

_____

_____

_____

_____

_____

_____

_____

_____

_____

_____

_____

_____

WRITE ABOUT HOW YOU CAN LEARN FROM THESE SITUATIONS. HOW CAN YOU CHANGE YOUR THOUGHTS FROM BEING SOMETHING THAT YOU CONSIDER AS A FAILURE VERSUS SOMETHING THAT YOU CAN LEARN AND GROW FROM?

_____

_____

_____

_____

_____

_____

_____

_____

_____

_____

_____

_____

_____

_____

_____

_____

_____

Embracing failure involves recognizing when to pivot away from goals that no longer serve your interests or values. Understanding what you've learned from the experience and why it's relevant or irrelevant is important. Clarity in decision-making is an essential part of your growth. I invite you to look at failure through a different lens. This mindset shift can prevent stagnation. There is no such thing as failure with the right mindset; there are only opportunities to learn and grow.

*Step 3: Celebrating Success*

Be intentional about your success. Success is best achieved by being clear, concise, and consistent. Where are you going? What is your destination? Set clear and actionable goals. What steps will you take each day to achieve your goals? Success isn't a one-size-fits-all. It's personal and varies from one individual to another.

## WHAT DOES IT LOOK LIKE FOR YOU?

_____

_____

_____

_____

_____

_____

_____

_____

_____

_____

_____

_____

_____

_____

_____

_____

_____

_____

_____

## WHAT DOES SUCCESS FEEL LIKE FOR YOU?

_____

_____

_____

_____

_____

_____

_____

_____

_____

_____

_____

_____

_____

_____

_____

_____

_____

_____

**DON'T COMPARE YOURSELF TO OTHERS. BE CLEAR ABOUT WHAT SUCCESS WILL MEAN TO YOU. TO ACHIEVE SUCCESS, YOU NEED CONCRETE STEPS. VISUALIZE AND TAKE ACTION. ASK YOURSELF:**

**ARE MY GOALS CLEAR AND REALISTIC?**

_____

_____

_____

_____

_____

_____

_____

_____

_____

_____

_____

_____

_____

_____

_____

_____

_____

# CAN MY GOALS BE MEASURED?

_____

_____

_____

_____

_____

_____

_____

_____

_____

_____

_____

_____

_____

_____

_____

_____

_____

_____

_____

## WHAT DAILY ACTIONS WILL I TAKE TO REACH MY GOALS?

_____

_____

_____

_____

_____

_____

_____

_____

_____

_____

_____

_____

_____

_____

_____

_____

_____

_____

_____

_____

Success also requires being specific. Vague goals and aspirations like "I want to be successful" lack direction. Believe in your ability to succeed and affirm your goals aspirations. For example, "My name is Katherine, and I am [state your goal]." Using an "I am" statement is affirmative and powerful. Commit to specific actions daily. You can achieve great things if you believe you can! Dream big and set goals.

# BE CLEAR, CONCISE, AND CONSISTENT

Celebrate all victories, even if they are small. Acknowledge your progress. The road to success is not always easy, but it is achievable. Stay focused, and do not get discouraged. **Remember the 3Cs: Be clear, concise, and consistent!** Continue to affirm your goals. Acknowledging every step of progress, especially celebrating when you overcome obstacles, is essential. Developing a growth mindset leads to resilience. This maintains motivation and momentum while encouraging personal and professional growth.

*Bringing It All Together: Fear, Failure, and Success*

By confronting your fears, embracing your failures, and celebrating your success, you are equipped with the three essential steps to make sustainable progress. This is a transition point - from fear to fulfillment, uncertainty to clarity, and stagnation to growth. If you have any self-limiting beliefs, you must address them before they negatively impact you and prevent you from achieving your dreams.

The letters you will begin to write are powerful. Fear, failure, and success are connected, forming a continuous personal development cycle. Confronting your fears opens the door to trying new things, which includes embracing failures, reshaping your thinking, and learning. This learning guides you to make informed choices and persevere or pivot towards more aligned goals, leading to successes worth celebrating.

Celebrating success is the manifestation of your goals. It's a personal commitment to your aspirations and plans. Be intentional and read your "Dear Success" letter after 30 days. When you read it, take a moment to be reminded of the progress made and the lessons learned. This letter is not just a message to your future self; it's a powerful tool for reflection, motivation, and continued growth.

The journey towards success is interconnected. Confronting fear sets the foundation for a mind-shift of growth. Embracing failure is not just about learning from mistakes but also about reassessing and realigning your goals. It's a critical step that informs your journey, helping you to focus on what truly matters.

Celebrating success, both as a reward and a motivator, is a reminder of your capabilities and a reinforcement of your commitment to your goals. Maintaining momentum and enthusiasm will help with resilience. Understanding these steps long-term is vital for a transformative journey, embracing resilience, adaptability, and nurturing self-awareness. Together, this forms a powerful strategy for personal and professional growth.

# Do's and Don't of Letters To Yourself

When writing, do what works best for you. Identify a time of day and place where you can be comfortable writing. If having a set time to write does not work well for you, make modifications and write when it meets your needs. Many people who enjoy nature write at a park or outside their homes. Some people write late at night. Others prefer early morning writing as soon as they wake up. There is no one way to write. You are in control, and you have the power to do what works best for you.

# THE DO'S

## BE B.R.A.V.E

*B*elieve that your thoughts matter. Be honest with yourself. If you don't know who you are, no one else will. Identify the setting where you are most comfortable and able to write freely. Believe that you can explore your thoughts. Believe that you can write a dynamic and inspirational letter to yourself.

*R*ealize that your thoughts, reflections, and ideas are the words that you need to hear that others will often never know. Sometimes, the first letters to ourselves are written to people who have hurt us. These letters often deal with emotions that challenge us. Keep writing.

*A*ccept where you are on your journey. If you don't accept who you are in your stage and place in life (your journey), no one else will. Do not feel pressured to share your letters with others. When you write without worrying about who will read it, you may find it easier to explore your truths.

*V*aliantly write. Being valiant means not giving up on writing to yourself and having courage. This can initially be challenging because you must accept and acknowledge your thoughts. When you focus on being valiant, you can write the most powerful letter you have ever written.

*E*xecute something new by trying to write a genuine and authentic letter. Set a time and determine when and how you will write. The most important part when you execute is to write and be honest with yourself. Just get started.

When you are B.R.A.V.E while writing, you allow yourself to create powerful, heartfelt reflections documenting growth. Sometimes, people share that when they wrote their first letter to themselves, they cried because they were transparently honest with their feelings of fear, failure, and success. If this happens to you, honor where you are in the process. Sometimes, looking back on these letters will inspire you and allow you to see where and how you have grown. This type of writing helps you never to get stagnant.

Writing a letter to yourself will allow you to acknowledge and accept that you are perfectly imperfect. You are who you were created to be. You have things that make you special that others do not understand. There are words that you need to hear that no one knows to tell you, so you should tell yourself. You must learn to empower yourself and be confident that you are now equipped with the skills you need to be the best version of yourself. You are about to walk into a new, incredible, and exciting journey, and it all begins with writing three powerful and impactful letters to yourself.

# Be R.E.A.L.

*R*emove external distractions. Close your eyes and think about the prompt that is given. There are only three that we will explore. Some people have shared that they enjoy thinking about the prompt and the related emotions to visualize situations related to their writing.

*E*xplore where you are in life at this moment. What lessons have you learned up to this point in your life? What experiences and defining moments have shaped your beliefs, emotions, and responses to situations?

*A*llow yourself to embrace the process of writing. No one will read your letter unless you share it with them. For this reason, you should be open and honest with yourself. Keep your letter safe if you choose not to share it.

*L*eave anything that does not serve your future well in the past. When you are done writing, don't be afraid to let go of past hurts, emotions, and feelings. Take this as a moment to meet the new you. Be encouraged and empowered that you may have experienced unpleasant things, but it does not mean these unpleasant experiences define your future.

Lastly, when writing these letters, I ask that you be open, honest, transparent, and vulnerable to explore prompts. I want you to write until you feel there is nothing else to write.

# THE DON'TS

## DON'T BE V.A.G.U.E

*V*ague letters are written when you are trying to hide your honest, transparent, and authentic thoughts. Being vague can be observed when letters are short, abstract, and unclear. Don't be vague. Explore the writing prompt.

*A*rgumentative letters without action can be unhealthy. Our actions, reactions, words, and body language don't always reflect our feelings. If past situations have you trapped in your thoughts, you may be led to begin your writing prompt by addressing that emotion. Once a situation has happened, you can acknowledge it, learn from it, and move forward.

Example

Below is a sample of an excerpt from the introduction and summary of the letter:

"Dear Fear, you have controlled me for many years; you made me feel less than the person I was created to be.... However, today, I will start a new chapter that does not include you etc..." In this excerpt from a letter, rather than being argumentative, the writer accepts and acknowledges every aspect of the journal prompt but ends with an empowering close rather than an argumentative one.

*G*uilty letters can force us to feel stagnant. Sometimes, we get trapped in the "what if" world. I define the "what if" world as the questions we ask ourselves when we try to replay and relive scenarios from the past that cannot be changed. Even in the most challenging scenarios of life, everything happens as it is meant to be. We can always learn from the most unpleasant and even unfathomable scenarios. Use the letter process to write, reflect, and release.

*U*ltimatums with yourself should always be avoided. Did you know that you can go back and revisit a letter? You can add and edit a letter because you own your thoughts and ideas. Don't put yourself in a situation where you feel you have failed to write the letter. There are no right or wrong answers.

*E*agerness to finish the letter may limit your personal growth. It is important not to be eager to finish quickly. When you write a letter to yourself and are limited in time, you risk limiting your reflection. The most important aspect is the quality of the letter and that it conveys what is most important to you. Have you written until you feel you have released fear and failures and are ready to envision your successful future self?

The type of letters I am encouraging you to write are the beginning of what can become a lifelong process of reflection for you. You may find that one day, many years from now, you will publish your letters in a book. Your letters contain memories from your life, your heartfelt emotions, and should never be rushed or viewed as an ending. Letters to yourself are always the beginning of new thoughts, ideas, and reflections. Never rush the process of committing to yourself.

*Summary*

Your letters are an extension of you. Each letter should explore the depth of your past, present, and future. Your letter should inspire you to release emotions and embrace the evolution of the magnificent person that you are.

You can do it!

You should do it!

I challenge you to start now.

Today is a great day to write.

As you begin, remember this is a private process that does not have to be shared with others unless you choose to. Writing can assist you in prioritizing your goals, dreams, and aspirations. In the same aspect, it can also be a method to tackle fears and concerns and identify when changes are needed in our lives. At any point in writing, if you feel that the issues you are dealing with are too overwhelming, it may be important to seek the health of a medical professional you trust, including physicians, counselors, or another trustworthy person.

Today, in fact, right now, begin the process of writing three letters to yourself. Start with one letter at a time. Some people can do this on the same day, while others may require additional time. Do what works best for you. What is most important is that you take the time to reflect, write, and, when needed, go back and revisit the questions and process of addressing the questions presented.

Before we explore what each letter will entail, let's discuss the process you should use when writing.

- You must remove external distractions.
- Explore where you are in life now.
- Allow yourself to embrace the writing process and leave anything that does not serve your present or future well in the past.

Write and keep writing.
You can do it.
Take time, pace yourself, and don't rush.

Many people have found it helpful to set a goal to write 3 paragraphs initially when they begin, but later, they find that they easily exceed this. If this method works for you, I encourage you to try it. Each following section begins with a prompt to write a letter to yourself. Take time to complete the questions and jot notes, and you begin to explore your thoughts. This helps you focus on your idea while having the courage to write each letter.

# DEAR FEAR

*N*ow it's time to apply what you have learned. The first letter is the dear fear letter. It is strategically placed first because fear can stagnate you if you don't have the courage to confront it. Remember, as you begin this letter, consider the part of yourself that no one knows. Even if you are confident, there are often parts of you that no one knows about, resulting in things you fear. Write down what you must tell yourself for this section. Again, this can be something internal that no one else knows except for you. Take a moment to reflect. What patterns do you find yourself repeating that are not healthy? Are there unhealthy coping mechanisms you utilize daily that are not beneficial to your success? Do you fear letting these habits go? Write this down. What are you afraid of? What is holding you back from achieving your dreams? Create a list of your top 10 fears. If you have less than 10 words, begin with the words or areas of your life that cause you to experience fear.

It is often said that fear begins in the mind. In this moment, I want you to name the fear, confront it, and feel confident in releasing it while acknowledging that it no longer controls you. When you think about the situations and thoughts that you experience that result in fear or a fear reaction, imagine what life would be like if you released those negative experiences from your mind. Is there anything in your life that needs to be excluded? Are there any negative habits, people, or situations you have control over but willingly allow yourself to be exposed to? If you faced your fear today and took back control of your life, what amazing things would you be able to accomplish?

*Take a moment to reflect*

**WHAT PATTERNS DO YOU FIND YOURSELF REPEATING THAT ARE NOT HEALTHY?**

ARE THERE UNHEALTHY COPING MECHANISMS
YOU UTILIZE DAILY THAT ARE NOT BENEFICIAL
TO YOUR SUCCESS? DO YOU FEAR LETTING
THESE HABITS GO? CONSIDER WHY.

_____

_____

_____

_____

_____

_____

_____

_____

_____

_____

_____

_____

_____

_____

_____

_____

_____

_____

## WHAT ARE YOU AFRAID OF? WHAT IS HOLDING YOU BACK FROM ACHIEVING YOUR DREAMS?

_____

_____

_____

_____

_____

_____

_____

_____

_____

_____

_____

_____

_____

_____

_____

_____

_____

_____

_____

*Create a list of your top 10 fears. If you have less than 10 words, begin with the words or areas of your life that cause you to experience fear.*

_____

_____

_____

_____

_____

_____

_____

_____

_____

_____

_____

_____

_____

_____

_____

_____

_____

*Now that you have explored these questions and are thinking about facing your fears, it is time to begin writing one of the most powerful letters you will write. Let's begin.*

*Beginning with the word "Dear Fear" write a letter to yourself. It is important that you embrace your power and control as you 1) write until you have addressed all of the words that you need to say to your fears and 2) release any fears that are holding you back in life.*

Dear Fear,

_____

_____

_____

_____

_____

_____

_____

_____

_____

_____

_____

# DEAR FAILURE

$\mathcal{I}$t's time to write your second letter, the Dear Failure letter. Not succeeding at something does not mean that you are a failure. It means you have learned something that you don't want to duplicate and possibly ways to do it differently.

What things do you feel you have been less than successful at? Explore areas of your life, including family, friends, work, school, organizations, self-esteem, etc. Take a moment to reflect. What are things that others have said to you that have left you feeling hurt?

Have you ever failed at something? Of course you have. We all have had moments of not being as successful as we want. It's called learning. Sometimes learning takes replication by repeating things more than once.

Replication is not bad. It means you are learning, unlearning, and relearning. Until you understand this, you may be in a space where you feel a sense of failure. Have the words of others reinforced the feeling that you felt when you engaged in something and did not result in the desired outcome? Are there places you have been where someone or something leaves you feeling emotionally drained or less than inspired where you cannot move past the memory?

*Take a moment to reflect.*

## WHAT ARE THINGS THAT OTHERS HAVE SAID TO YOU THAT HAVE LEFT YOU FEELING HURT?

_____

_____

_____

_____

_____

_____

_____

_____

_____

_____

_____

_____

_____

_____

_____

_____

_____

_____

_____

# HAVE YOU EVER FAILED AT SOMETHING?

## HAVE THE WORDS OF OTHERS REINFORCED THE FEELING THAT YOU FELT WHEN YOU ENGAGED IN SOMETHING AND DID NOT RESULT IN THE DESIRED OUTCOME?

_____

_____

_____

_____

_____

_____

_____

_____

_____

_____

_____

_____

_____

_____

_____

_____

_____

_____

**ARE THERE PLACES YOU HAVE BEEN WHERE SOMEONE OR SOMETHING LEAVES YOU FEELING EMOTIONALLY DRAINED OR LESS THAN INSPIRED WHERE YOU CANNOT MOVE PAST THE MEMORY?**

_____

_____

_____

_____

_____

_____

_____

_____

_____

_____

_____

_____

_____

_____

_____

_____

_____

_____

_____

_____

*With all of these emotions in mind, take a moment to pause, then begin your letter. The first two words should begin with "Dear Failure"; however, the ending is whatever you decide. There are no correct or incorrect answers to your writing that anyone else can tell you. The words that you know that you need to hear are the correct words. The words that you do not want to include are the incorrect words. I only ask that you be honest with yourself and commit to writing an open and honest letter to yourself.*

Dear Failure,

_____

_____

_____

_____

_____

_____

_____

_____

_____

_____

# DEAR SUCCESS

Success is such a powerful word. There is someone, some experience, or something that defined what the initial image of success looked like for you. You have written two letters to yourself at this point in our time together. I hope you are learning, reflecting, and writing and have come to a new understanding by completing your Dear Fear and Failure letters. Now, I would like you to consider success. After you write this letter, I encourage you to mail it yourself within 30 days. You will be inspired by receiving words of encouragement perfectly written just for you. Speak positive words of aspiration in the success letter. It is important to consider where you see yourself in five (5) years and the next 30 days. It is often said that it takes 30 days to form a habit. What do you need to accomplish in the next 30 days to build the foundation to form good habits to achieve your long-term goals?

You were created for a purpose. There are ideas that you have that can only be manifested by you. As you consider the word success, "you can do it" and "you were created to do amazing things." Although you may not hear this often enough, "You can do it." You have the power within you to achieve everything that your heart desires. In many instances, achieving your goals, dreams, and aspirations to achieve success begins with an idea or thought, putting the thought into writing, writing goals, and establishing the steps required for goal attainment. This final letter is all about you. Don't limit yourself or your dreams. From words of inspiration to congratulating yourself in advance for all of the wonderful things you will do, this letter is very important for you to complete. Take a moment to reflect. What are your goals and aspirations?

Identify three short-term goals that you have for yourself. These can be in health, personal development, professional development, career, family, etc... Where do you see yourself in 30 days if you complete your goals? What will you have accomplished if you achieve your goals? What words of encouragement do you need to hear that others rarely say to you? What do you know about yourself that others don't know?

Now that you have started to reflect upon your future success, write a letter to your future self as it relates to success. Don't try to minimize the vision that you have for yourself. Think about the advice you would want to hear or even the advice you would have given yourself in previous years. Be encouraged and inspired to do amazing things, and you write the Dear Success letter to yourself.

*Take time to reflect.*

**WHAT ARE YOUR GOALS AND ASPIRATIONS?**

_____

_____

_____

_____

_____

_____

_____

_____

_____

_____

_____

_____

_____

_____

_____

_____

_____

_____

_____

_____

IDENTIFY THREE SHORT-TERM GOALS THAT YOU
HAVE FOR YOURSELF. THESE CAN BE IN
HEALTH, PERSONAL DEVELOPMENT, PROFES-
SIONAL DEVELOPMENT, CAREER, FAMILY, ETC...
WHERE DO YOU SEE YOURSELF IN 30 DAYS IF
YOU COMPLETE YOUR GOALS? WHAT WILL YOU
HAVE ACCOMPLISHED?

_____

_____

_____

_____

_____

_____

_____

_____

_____

_____

_____

_____

_____

_____

_____

_____

**WHAT WORDS OF ENCOURAGEMENT DO YOU NEED TO HEAR THAT OTHERS RARELY SAY TO YOU? WHAT DO YOU KNOW ABOUT YOURSELF THAT OTHERS DON'T KNOW?**

_____

_____

_____

_____

_____

_____

_____

_____

_____

_____

_____

_____

_____

_____

_____

_____

_____

_____

*Now that you have started to reflect upon your future success, write a letter to your future self as it relates to success. Think about the advice you would want to hear or even the advice you would have given yourself in previous years. Be encouraged and inspired to do amazing things, and you write the Dear Success letter to yourself.*

Dear Success,

_____

_____

_____

_____

_____

_____

_____

_____

_____

_____

_____

_____

_____

_____

# You Can Succeed

Throughout this process of reflection and writing, you have explored your fear, failure, and success. You have learned how to be B.R.A.V.E while avoiding being V.A.G.U.E. Lastly, you have learned the R.E.A.L. writing method. This process is something that you should repeat on multiple occasions. When you don't reflect honestly by addressing your fears, overcoming failures, and focusing on success, you may feel alone.

We often want to be accepted by others for who we are when we do not first take the time to understand who we truly are or who we want to be. Writing a letter to ourselves enables us to understand who we are, who we have become, and who we want to be.

Many people suffer in silence between wanting to be accepted by others before they have accepted themselves. Whether you have experienced low self-esteem, overcome depression, loss, grief, guilt, or bullying, are a survivor of unhealthy relationships and interactions, or maybe none of these are true for you, as you write, remember that if you are here reading this, you are a champion and that you have a purpose.

If you write a letter to fear in the coming months, be sure to write a letter to failure and encourage yourself by writing a letter to your success to embrace and encourage yourself.

This is not a one-time process. Did you know you will need to address fear, failure, and success more than once in life? I am excited about this for you. Here's the exciting part: You have just learned an important lesson. That lesson is understanding that fear is part of the process as long as you do not allow yourself to become stagnated.

Did you know that failure is also part of the process you will experience many times in life? You may be asking, why would someone be excited about failure. Failure means that you are learning, unlearning, and relearning. Failure is part of the process because it means you are growing by trying new things. If you are learning, it means that you are alive and you are growing.

Growth is an essential contributing factor required for your success in life. If you do not fail, it may mean that you are not stretching yourself or evolving as the person you can truly be. If you think of failing as falling, think of success as standing up. When the gravity of life pulls you down, you must find the strength and courage to get back up. Success is getting back up.

We all have unsuccessful moments. Reflecting on these moments can help understand what went well and how to improve in the future. Reflecting on failure can also help you understand when there are people, situations, organizations, or environments in which you have placed yourself that may be unhealthy, unproductive, and no longer serve you well. Writing a letter to your success allows you to take a moment and see yourself in the environment you desire.

Writing is a way for you to empower yourself. Today, I hope that this is the first of many days that you will write a letter to yourself as you move past your pain, fears, and difficult situations until you release anything that does not serve the new you well.

Your life matters.
You matter.
Be B.R.A.V.E
Don't be V.A.G.U.E
And always be R.E.A.L. with yourself.

Honor where you are in your life's journey and know that in this moment, you are also becoming equipped to thrive. You can do it.

# Bonus Letters

# LETTER

_____

_____

_____

_____

_____

_____

_____

_____

_____

_____

_____

_____

_____

_____

_____

_____

_____

_____

# LETTER

_____

_____

_____

_____

_____

_____

_____

_____

_____

_____

_____

_____

_____

_____

_____

_____

_____

# LETTER

# LETTER

_____

_____

_____

_____

_____

_____

_____

_____

_____

_____

_____

_____

_____

_____

_____

_____

_____

_____

# LETTER

_____

_____

_____

_____

_____

_____

_____

_____

_____

_____

_____

_____

_____

_____

_____

_____

_____

_____

_____

_____

# LETTER

_____

_____

_____

_____

_____

_____

_____

_____

_____

_____

_____

_____

_____

_____

_____

_____

_____

_____

_____

# LETTER

_____

_____

_____

_____

_____

_____

_____

_____

_____

_____

_____

_____

_____

_____

_____

_____

_____

_____

_____

# LETTER

_____

_____

_____

_____

_____

_____

_____

_____

_____

_____

_____

_____

_____

_____

_____

_____

_____

_____

_____

_____

# LETTER

_____

_____

_____

_____

_____

_____

_____

_____

_____

_____

_____

_____

_____

_____

_____

_____

_____

_____

_____

_____

_____

# LETTER

# LETTER

# LETTER

www.ingramcontent.com/pod-product-compliance
Lightning Source LLC
Chambersburg PA
CBHW051005140626
46546CB00016B/876